MORGAN'S CROWN

By Morgan Colen & Maxine Galloway
Illustrated by Mauricio Paillacho

Printed in the United States of America

First Printing, 2020

ISBN: 978-0-578-81432-2

Published by PurposefulTime, LLC
www.purposefultime.com

Dedication & Special Acknowledgments

In 2015, Morgan's hair loss began. As a parent, I wanted to protect her from public scrutiny and bullying, while I sought every possible solution for a cure. During my daughter's transformational journey, I maximized on opportunities to highlight her inner beauty. I am proud of who she has become. I find joy in seeing her lift her head high and boldly share her experiences with the world. This Alopecian princess has blossomed with confidence and purpose. Her most admired philanthropic work entails creating and donating handmade couture crowns.

"Morgan's Crown" is an empowering and inspirational reminder to all little girls that you are royalty. So, reclaim your "crown" (self-esteem and confidence)!.

This book is dedicated to my 1st grade teacher, Ms. Jaleesa Ramsey who believed in me and is solely credited for my participation in the Little Miss Rockbridge Pageant. Thank you also to all teachers for your time, resources, and encouragement, which enables students to achieve their dreams.

Thank you to my parents, Maxine and Rick, for your love and support. To my siblings: Makhai (Thank you for adding your artistic talent to the illustrations in my book), Aziza, Lanier and Jacob; grandparents, the Late Mr. Morgan Colen, Jean Colen, Alfred and Violet Galloway; aunts & uncles, Marquita ("Aunty Kitty", thank you for reviewing and critiquing my book) and Miranda Galloway, Stephanie & Eric Brown; , the late Jeffrey Colen and Regine Colen and Terry & Patricia Colen, cousins, Dr. Carrine Todman-Lewis (thank you for your assistance with reviewing and editing this book), Drew & Roslyn Colen, Marquel, Roshonna, Myasia, Kimiah and a host of cousins, too many to name!); my church family at the Tabernacle of the Lord Church and former church New Bethlehem Baptist Church and a host of family and friends (too numerous to mention) you uplift me and make me feel beautiful the way God created me. To all of the moms and dads that remind their little girls that they are royal, you are special!. Lastly, to all of the little girls reading this book, know that you are unique, you are beautiful, and you have what it takes to win!!.

Hi! I'm Morgan. I have
Alopecia.
This is how you say it...
Ah-lo-pee-sha!
Funny word, right?
It's the reason I don't have
hair.

I wasn't born with Alopecia. As a baby, I had thick, long hair that took hours to comb through and it hurt. "Ouch!" I often cried. So, my mom would try to be as gentle as she could.

When I was three years old, I became very sick with a high fever. It caused my body to attack my hair follicles and my hair started to fall out in patches.

My parents took me to see many different doctors to try to stop the hair loss. We tried, ointments, shampoos, sprays but nothing worked.

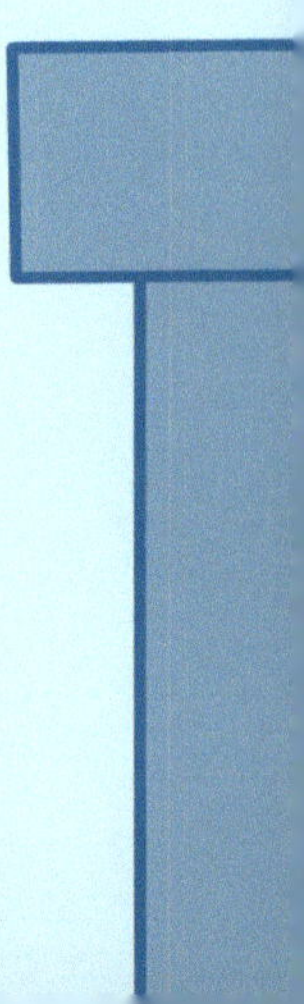

Mommy would say, “Morgie, do you know that your hair is your crown? I didn’t know what she meant, so I asked, “Do you mean the kind a princess wear?”. “Yes!” she replied, “and you’re my little princess, so put your chin up before your crown slips”. This always made me feel better.

After a while, almost all of my hair had fallen out, leaving only one small piece in the front. It looked like a bare tree in winter.

My mom sadly decided to cut it off to match the rest of my head. I felt my bald head. My crown was gone!, I turned to my mom frantically and said, “Mommy, my crown slipped! Am I still a princess without my hair?”, Mom lifted my chin, looked me straight in the eyes, smiled, and said, “Of course, you are still a princess! You’re beautiful with or without hair. **So, be bold, be fierce, and BE-YOU-tiful!”.**

However, without my crown, I lost my confidence to play outside and meet new friends. So, I stayed home and played with my brother. At school, I wore hats so that people wouldn't stare at me.

I loved to dance, but when it was time for us to wear our hair in a bun, I felt left out without my crown. “I don’t want to dance anymore, Mommy!”. I cried, after my turban nearly slipped a few times while dancing.

Then, one day at school, I saw a flyer for the school pageant. The winner would get a bright, sparkling, new crown!. I hurried home.

“Mommy! Mommy!, guess what?!, there’s a pageant at my school and the winner gets a crown!, do you think I could win?”. My mom replied, “of course you can!. Remember, all you have to do is **be bold, be fierce, BE-YOU-tiful!”**.

Miss
Rockbridge
&
Little Miss
Rockbridge
Pageant

That night, as mom tucked me in, she read the story of Cinderella. I fell asleep imagining what it would be like to win a crown. But when I woke up, I felt my head and realized it was all a dream.

“But mom”, I said: “what about my hair?!, I can’t win without my hair!, everyone will laugh at me”. “Don’t you worry!, you just focus on your talent and I’ll help with the rest!”; she said reassuringly.

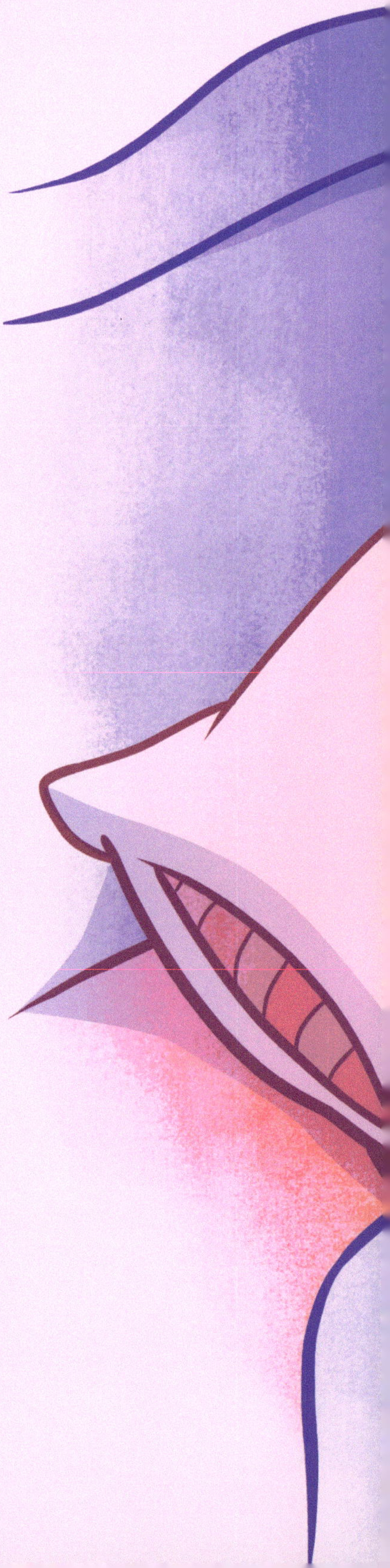

On the day before the pageant, mommy had a surprise for me. She took me to a special salon for children without hair to have a wig made just for me!; I loved my new hair!.

The next day, I woke up feeling excited!, "it's pageant day!". When we arrived at the school, there were families talking excitedly as they filled the auditorium. Backstage, our moms had so much fun getting us ready for the opening dance. We got to wear makeup, take pictures together and we wished each other good luck!. We all lined up to do the opening dance and introduction. Everyone wore matching red dresses.

I wowed the judges with my bright smile and confident voice, speaking in both French and English. “Bonjour! Je mapel Morgan, and I am in the first grade!”. The crowd cheered!.

Up next was the fun wear segment. I wore a unicorn skirt with a matching custom crown headband, a denim jacket, and custom sneakers with my name on them. My mom changed my hair style too. I twirled and skipped into the song, “Girls just wanna have fun!”.
I felt my self-confidence coming back!.

MORGAN

The big moment was finally here, the talent segment!. A hush fell over the crowd, as the lights were dimmed. The only lights shining were the lights that blinked on my silver rocket costume. I wore a bedazzled futuristic crown with a light beam. My leotard had sparkling gems on it and my skirt looked like a globe with continents on it. The crowd was wowed by my cardboard rocket, with cloth flames at the bottom. Smoke came from the bottom making it look real!. My voice could be heard on the speakers, as I counted down to take off in French. The crowd counted in English 3, 2, 1!, the music started and I twirled to the beat of: “Girls run the world!”; the crowd went crazy and my mom looked super proud!.

The evening gown segment was next. The pageant was nearing the end.
My mom sensed that I was nervous and whispered:
"Be bold, be fierce, be BE-YOU-tiful!".

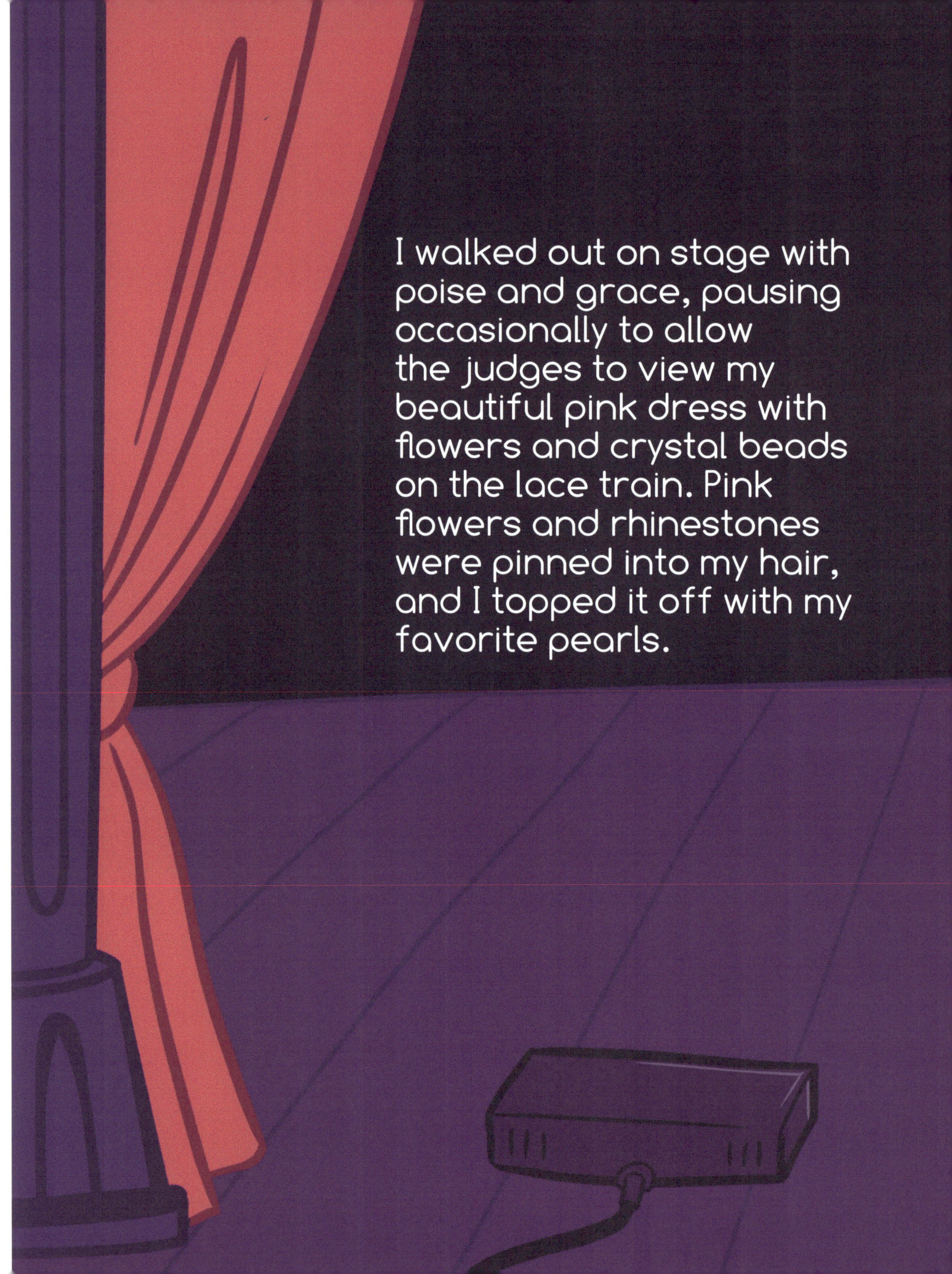

I walked out on stage with poise and grace, pausing occasionally to allow the judges to view my beautiful pink dress with flowers and crystal beads on the lace train. Pink flowers and rhinestones were pinned into my hair, and I topped it off with my favorite pearls.

Finally, it was time to announce the winner!. The competition was close!. The names of the second and first runner up were called, and there was only one spot left. I glanced over at my mom, shrugged and thought to myself, "I did my best"...

The crowd hushed and held their breath... AND THE WINNER OF LITTLE MISS ROCKBRIDGE IIIIIIIIIIIISSSSSSS... **"MISS MORGAN!!!".**

The crowd cheered!, I looked at my mom and couldn't believe it!, "I won!, I really won!". Mommy was right, I had what it took to win on the inside. **I just needed to be fierce, be bold and be myself!.**
I was draped with a sash, given roses, trophies and lastly; a big, bright, sparkly, new, beautiful CROWN!.

That night my mom asked, "How does it feel to be a princess, Morgie?", I paused and said: **"I was already a princess with or without a crown!".**

MORGAN'S CROWN

www.ingramcontent.com/pod-product-compliance
Ingram Content Group UK Ltd.
Pitfield, Milton Keynes, MK11 3LW, UK
UKHW061032310726
14089UKWH00009B/209
* 9 7 8 0 5 7 8 8 1 4 3 2 2 *